*LIFE
HAPPENS!*

LIFE HAPPENS!

How to navigate through life's challenges

WRITTEN BY ANITA A. FLAGG

XULON PRESS

Xulon Press
555 Winderley Pl, Suite 225
Maitland, FL 32751
407.339.4217
www.xulonpress.com

xulon PRESS

© 2024 by Anita A. Flagg

All rights reserved solely by the author. The author guarantees all contents are original and do not infringe upon the legal rights of any other person or work. No part of this book may be reproduced in any form without the permission of the author.

Due to the changing nature of the Internet, if there are any web addresses, links, or URLs included in this manuscript, these may have been altered and may no longer be accessible. The views and opinions shared in this book belong solely to the author and do not necessarily reflect those of the publisher. The publisher therefore disclaims responsibility for the views or opinions expressed within the work.

Unless otherwise indicated, Scripture quotations taken from the New King James Version (NKJV). Copyright © 1982 by Thomas Nelson, Inc. Used by permission. All rights reserved

Unless otherwise indicated, Scripture quotations taken from the King James Version (KJV)–*public domain.*

Paperback ISBN-13: 979-8-86850-397-9
Ebook ISBN-13: 979-8-86850-398-6

Dedication

I first want to thank my Lord and Savior for being with me on this journey called Life and for inspiring me to use my gift of writing! I'd also like to dedicate this book to husband Bishop Mark Flagg for the push to complete this work and to not give up on the vision for it! And to my daughters Candace L. Mumphrey and Christian L. Mumphrey for being my sweet inspirations from birth on through adulthood and for loving me through everything. I love you all!

Introduction

Have you ever arrived at a place in your life where things seemingly were moving right along and on track, so to speak? Then suddenly, the sound of abruptness fills your internal and external atmosphere due to the unexpected twist and turns that brings your entire life to a halt? The place that you thought you were at now becomes questionable and your place of contentment is now dissipated, housing in your heart pain, disappointment, and discouragement.

Adapting to the circumstances that have been dropped into one's lap which devastatingly changes everything is not easy! Every human being will inevitably come face to face with unforeseen, life-altering, life-changing situations that may detour them temporarily and even sometimes permanently. Some may experience the death of a loved one or the loss of a marriage, job, relationship, or friendship. Others may be subjected to hearing the news of an incurable disease or undergo a major financial interruption. Whatever the case, there is no more horrific feeling in all of the world than that of "hopelessness".

Hopelessness makes one weary and fearful as well as corrupts good thoughts and the ability to have a healthy mindset. It causes the soul to feel disparity and the mind to forget about what was and what could be, left to only focus on what is. It paralyzes the mind and body, and if it were to have its way, it would steal one's joy, hopes, and dreams, suck all life out, and ultimately destroy you.

CHAPTER 1

This Caught Me Off Guard

The most amazing thing about life are the new days, those days that God grants us with. With each new day comes new beginnings, limitless possibilities, and opportunities to be greeted with new mindsets as well as being the grantee of God's new puddles of mercy. Afterall, life is a gift in which we are to enjoy and live out to the fullest. No one asks to be born, but it is not up to us to decide on our fate or future. Life begins when we are born into the families chosen for us. It is Jeremiah 1:5 (AMP) that says, *Before I formed you in the womb I knew you [and approved of you as My chosen instrument], and before you were born I consecrated you [to Myself as My own]; I have appointed you as a prophet to the nations.*

Do you believe that God knows our future and what is ahead of us? He does! Nothing comes as a surprise to Him. We are the only ones who are shocked by situations that tend to catch us off guard. Life happens to us all. Situations can either make us or break us into many pieces, leaving us to wonder what has happened. Many times, when storms hit home base, they have the propensity to change the entire trajectory of our life. Changing positions and direction is never easy for anyone, but change will happen to everyone. People will change, friend circles will change, physical appearances will change, individuals and lifestyles will change, and seasons will change.

There are many things in life that will not shock us, but there are things that will turn our lives upside down. For instance, it is normal to hit a "bump in the road." It is also typical throughout our lifetime to have a few strong winds blow our way as well as have a few rain clouds hang low. However, there are winds that suddenly appear that are completely unexpected; this is the wind that changes everything!

As I recall this time in my life, I had endured many trials and tests, as many of us do. I'd suffered some things physically, had been tested with financial issues, had some employment challenges, and was making great attempts overall to grow past my own personal pain. Growing past my pain was easy if I stayed focused on what God's *Word* said regarding me. I not only believed God's Word, I had to put it into action regarding my life, children, and relationships.

Putting God's Word into action was not always easy depending on where I was in my soulish realm. When I say soulish realm, I am speaking of our will, intellect, and emotions, which, unfortunately many times, can be moved by what and how we feel. Being moved by our emotions (especially negative ones) will make us lose sight of our purpose and destiny as well as God's amazing plan for our lives. God has promised us a destined end; one that we could never imagine or fathom.

The next few winds that blew in my direction were totally life-changing; after all, the purpose of wind blowing in certain seasons are designed to do one thing, to scatter seed that will eventually take root in the ground and grow in their due season! I had become used to winds blowing my way before; nevertheless, one wind that blew almost wiped me out. Why would I say that? Because its true! I would manage to control, for the most part, my own feelings and how strongly they wanted to dictate to me the what's, how's, when's, and whys concerning my life. I had settled within myself that this was how life was meant to be. Wrong! I was not thinking very clearly. As a matter of fact, my vision had become clouded by the wind and the small particles of dust that found its way into my spiritual eyes, impeding my ability to see. I felt as if everything I knew to be a part of me was hijacked. What I am saying is that the definition of hijack, according to the dictionary, means to "unlawfully seize, in transit and force it to go into a different destination or use it for one's own purpose". Dictionary.com What I am really referring to is a spiritual hijacking.

Spiritually, I was held up and forced into a different way of living and functioning. My life was not just in turmoil, but in some sense, the direction I believed I was going in was redirected. I felt lost! There was nothing that anyone could say or do to assist me in getting past all the feelings that were tormenting me! I kept asking myself how I got here. I knew things were bad, but I didn't know that I'd be knocked off my feet and flat on my back spiritually. The blowing, howling winds did not come to play; in fact, they changed my life situations in the blink of an eye and the snap of a finger. The thief had come, and you know what thieves do; they take items that do not belong to them and use them for self-gain, dividend, and attainment.

That day, the thief came and ransacked my life with intents to kill all involved! My life was changed suddenly. Everything about my life and those attached to me shifted, causing a great collapse! One definition of collapse, when used as a noun, is "an instance of a structure falling out or in". Dictionary.com, (Online Site, 1995) So, what's structure? Used as a verb, structure is "to construct or to arrange according to a plan; give a pattern to or organization to". Webster, Noah, Merriam Webster Dictionary, 1806)

What I'm really saying is that the winds howled and blew vehemently to the point that my structured life, in appearance, fell apart. Some people walked out of my life while others gracefully made an entrance. Life was different. I had a difficult time deciphering between those who were trying to take advantage of the vulnerability that they'd sniffed out and those who were really on assignment from the Lord to help bring restoration back to me. Trouble was flooding my space, and I unintentionally gave way to the thieves' objectives.

> *The thief does not come except to steal, and to kill, and to destroy. I have come that they may have life, and that they may have it more abundantly.* John 10:10 (NKJV)

In hindsight, the things that happened were already in existence because things don't go wrong, they simply started off wrong. Honestly, by the time it was evident that my wrong start had caught up with me, I was at a place of utter fatigue, intense pain, and despair. I don't recall when everything came crashing down, but they did. Let me explain when I suggest that things started off wrong. People believe that things take a turn for the worst abruptly in their lives when, in fact, there were signs given for the sole purpose of giving insight to a situation or individual. We always get warning signs. For example, an abuser will not just suddenly abuse after marriage or after the beginning of a new relationship, they, with subtleties, will abuse and control the mind of the abused while dating. Many of us do not want to see warning signs because we choose to ignore them for various reasons, but it does not mean that they are not there.

I, too, have ignored warning signs. Frankly, I allowed my own insecurities and not having a father in my life walk me right into a situation that I would eventually have to make some profoundly serious life-changing decisions to get out of. I was at a place in which it was difficult to withstand the effects of the pain I was experiencing. I made many attempts to make it go away by numbing it, but it did not matter what I did to try to stop the pain, it did not go anywhere. This pain of disappointment, shame, rejection, abandonment, and lies was felt in every part of my being. It was painful to breathe, to walk, to move, to smile or laugh, to cry, or to even exist. I attempted to escape the pain that had taken me over, but I did not know how to do it without causing more damage.

As I have healed throughout the past six years, I realize that the pain was never intended to destroy me, but rather to grow me! The pain was purposeful. As brutal as it was at times, it was really working for my good.

> *And we know [with great confidence] that God [who is deeply concerned about us] causes all things to work together [as a plan] for good for those who love God, to those who are called according to His plan and purpose.* Romans 8:28 (AMP)

What I couldn't comprehend then I am able to comprehend now. I was taught growing up in church that you do not question God's business, yet I recall questioning God about my condition and state of being. I broke every rule because I asked God many questions, as I believed He was the only one who could answer them. I wanted to know if I was going to die in that state. I wondered if anyone could see me and feel my pain. I asked God if I was going to recover. I asked Him if my life would ever be the same. The answers to all of my questions were emphatically, "No," at least that is what I told myself.

Even so, God assured me in my discomfort that things were going to change for the better. I just did not see how things improving for me was possible. I was scarcely breathing and drowning in my own sorrow, but I know that it was God's grace, love, and power that was going to push me through to the other side where "better" awaited me! To be frank, I was just not prepared for such a strong wind to blow my way. Of course, I had had winds blow in storms, but not on this level. These winds were fierce and identically strong. As fierce as the storms were, my spiritual armor was my complete protection in hindsight. I took a hit and that caused massive damage.

Chapter 2

Time Tells All

Its amazing to me how we tend to walk haphazardly through life. We take many things for granted; not always intentionally, but we do. We blindly walk through life many times and don't always look at things through the eyes of God; rather, we use our own sight to navigate through God's earth. How reckless is that?

Here's the issue with trying to walk by sight rather than by faith. God never intended for us to get through life on our own abilities. We are fragile beings and not smart enough to know what to do or when to do it. We must trust our Manufacturer, Maker, and Creator.

> *But without faith it is impossible to [walk with God and] please Him, for whoever comes [near] to God must necessarily believe that God exists and that He rewards those who [earnestly and diligently] seek Him.*
>
> Hebrews 11:6 [AMP]

If we are not careful to rely on God for everything, we'll continue tripping up over our mistakes, carelessness, and failures. We will walk into life situations blindly and not see them coming at all. Be that as it may, we need God to guide us through this thing called "life" because, with time and in time, we will learn to trust our God redo and undo some things, but I couldn't because time kept moving even though I had stopped. There will be times is our lives when we desire to have a redo or a do-over, and sometimes they are necessary. Nevertheless, while I couldn't go back, I was finally moving forward because God redeemed time for me.

One thing that must be understood is that life happens to all and there is no need to be shocked when situations change, when people change how they feel about you, when marriages fall apart, when health conditions in our bodies turn for the worse, when jobs are terminated, when we suffer financial loss, or when children go the total opposite of what they were taught. This is called the inevitable. This means that life happenings are certain to happen, for sure to happen, are unavoidable, unpreventable, or fated. Time brings with it transitions. A transition is the process of a period of changing from one state to another. Murray, James Sir. (A New English Dictionary on Historical Principals, 1879) Really, our lives are always in constant transition until, ultimately, change takes its proper place. There is a song I am reminded of hearing as a child, "Hold to God's Unchanging Hand" by Jennie Wilson (1906). What an amazing song filled with words of positivity and power I recall! The first stanza if the song is powerful and filled with positivity. This song brings back so many memories hearing it as a child but never fully comprehending it until I became an adult who was facing many some challenges in life.

It is the first six words of the first stanza that I want to put emphasis on. It is time that is filled with swift, rapid, sudden, prompt, immediate, or unhesitating movements. Think about it. There are ups, downs, in, outs, rollercoaster rides, smooth sailing, turbulence, peaks, and valleys in this thing called life in which every situation that comes, whether good or bad, happens when time says it is time. Time is filled with movement and transition, which can sometimes result in pain and joys that have not been experienced. We have all been there;

we have all hurt to the point where it felt as if the pain would never dissipate.

I am reminded of the first account noted that Jesus began feeling pain in the Garden of Gethsemane. It was unbearable and to the point where when He prayed, the Bible records that it was as if He sweated drops of blood:

> *Then Jesus came with them to a place called Gethsemane (olive press), and He told His disciples, "Sit here while I go over there and pray." And taking with Him Peter and the two sons of Zebedee (James and John), He began to be grieved and greatly distressed. Then He said to them, "My soul is deeply grieved, so that I am almost dying of sorrow. Stay here and stay awake and keep watch with Me." And after going a little farther, He fell face down and prayed, saying, "My father, if it is possible [that is, consistent with Your will], let this cup pass from Me; yet not as I will, but as You will.* Matthew 26:36-39 (AMP)

We can all learn from Jesus's approach to His "Gethsemane/Golgotha" experience. Firstly, with what little strength He had left, He was able to pray. Secondly, He was relinquished His will and emotions, which, at the time, were fear and distress to His God in order to complete the assignment that was approaching Him. The time had come and there was no turning back because time was not on His side. Time is the only thing that grows us, heals us, strengthens us, and teaches us life lessons!

When my children were younger, I had posted a poem on the wall in the hallway of our home that I got when I went out of town for a conference about time ("I have only just a minute" by Benjamin E. Mays). Mays, Benjamin. I Have Only Just a Minute, 2016. I chose the hallway because the bedrooms were located there, and they were what He would experience for most of His short life here on Earth. When the day finally arrived and it was time for the biggest test that He would ever face to happen, He Himself asked, "Why?"

> *About the ninth hour Jesus cried out with a loud [agonized]voice, "Eli, Eli, lama sabachthani?" that is, "My God, My God, why have you forsaken me?"*
>
> Matthew 27:46 (AMP)

His wailing out to His Father because of the agony, pain, fear, and loneliness that He was feeling cannot compare to some of the tribulations and tests that we go through in our lifetime. Unfortunately for us, we have no clue as to when misfortunes, hiccups, falls, blunders, sicknesses, job losses, family changes, betrayals, scandals, or anything considered to be a crisis is coming our way. Still, it does not stop them from coming!

Do you and I really understand what a "crisis" is? Do we really understand how crises can and do affect us as well as the long-term effect they can have? According to Protocol, "a crisis is defined as an unstable or crucial time or state of affairs in which a decisive change is impending." It is also "a situation that has reached a critical stage, one with the distinct possibility of highly undesirable outcome." Murray, James Sir. (A New English Dictionary on Historical Principals, The Oxford Dictionary, 1879) In other words, a crisis will take us from normalcy to unnormal within a matter of seconds. Crises causes those who experience them to live below their accustomed way of living. Job loss, divorce, unwanted pregnancy, death, scandal, sickness, family dissension, sudden loss, and so much more will and do lead people of all walks of life into crisis. I have great news, though! Jesus Christ is Lord of crisis!

Now of this writing, the world is in a colossal crisis. It is one of the biggest I have seen in my lifetime. We are amid a pandemic and millions of lives have been lost as well as jobs, and businesses and families have been severely affected by this. The world has changed and what we knew to be normal before the crisis is now in the past. We all have had to adapt to a "new norm" because the situation that caused the crisis to be reached a critical phase in which things had to change.

> *Apostle Paul went through a life-altering crisis, one in which his life would be different forever. Acts chapter nine is where then Saul became or was converted to Paul. Verse one says " Now Saul, still breathing threats and murder against the disciples of the Lord and relentless in his search for believers, went to the high priest, and he asked for letters of authority from him to the synagogues at Damascus, so that if he found any men or women there belonging to the way believers, followers of Jesus the Messiah, men and women alike, he could arrest them and bring them bound with chains to Jerusalem. As he traveled, he approached Damascus, and suddenly a light from heaven flashed around him [displaying the glory and majesty of Christ]; and he fell to the ground and heard a voice saying to him, Saul, Saul, why are your persecuting and oppressing me? And Saul said, who are You, Lord? And he answered, I am Jesus who you are persecuting, now get up and go into the city, and you will be told what you must do. The men who were traveling with him (were terrified and stood speechless, hearing the voice but seeing no one. Saul got up from the ground, but though his eyes were open, he could not see nothing; so, they led him by the hand and brough him into Damascus. And he was unable to see for three days, and he neither ate nor drank.*

Now in Damascus there was a disciple named Ananias; and the Lord said to him a vision, Ananias, and he answered, Here I am, Lord. And the Lord said to him get up and go to the street called Straight and ask at the house of Judas for a man from Tarsus named Saul; for he is praying there, and in a vision, he has seen a man named Ananias come in and place his hands on him, so that he may regain his sight. But Ananias answered, Lord, I have heard from many people about this, especially how much suffering and evil he has brough on your saints (God's people) at Jerusalem; and here in Damascus he has authority from the high priests to put in chains all who call on Your name confessing you as Savior. But the Lord said to him, Go, for this man is a deliberately chosen instrument of Mine, to bear my name before the Gentiles and Kings and the sons of Israel. For I will make clear to him how much he must suffer and endure for my name's sake. Immediately something like scales fell from Saul's eyes and he regained his sight Then he got up and was baptized; and he took some food and was strengthened. Acts 9:1-18 (AMP)

The trial that Saul faced on the Damascus Road changed the very course of his life. It was unexpected. The timing was not necessarily the best. He lost his physical sight temporarily to gain spiritual sight permanently. Saul never expected such a crisis to appear, but it did, and that is generally how it goes. We never run into crisis like we do old friends and neighbors from around the neighborhood. No! Crises run into us full speed ahead and, most times, we do not see them coming.

So, if you are thinking about when the timing for a crisis is ever good, its not; however, when they do appear, they alter our lives, set us on a different course, rearrange things around us, have the propensity to change the dynamics in our families, may lead to job loss, financial interruptions, or may just cause debilitation for a considerable amount of time. The good thing about a crisis is that it does not stay; it eventually makes its way down the street or around the corner to change the lives of others.

Never allow the thought of a crisis put fear in your heart! The fact is that crises build us, mature us, grow us, teach us, give us stamina, and show us what we are made of! While there may not be a good time for crisis to come, there's always a good time for faith to grow and it most certainly grows when we allow God's Positioning System (GPS) guide us and lead us into the places He desires for us and knows that they are better for us!

Chapter 4

God's Positioning System (GPS)

As I think about moments in time that I had no idea where I was going, how I was getting there, and what I was to do with the challenges that had pretty much been dumped in my lap (life), I cannot help but rejoice and get excited about the fact that it was only God who kept me, loved me through everything, and guided me on my journey that, by the way, took many detours only to get me to the place where I am today. I know without a shadow of a doubt that God's navigation system is by far the absolute greatest when it comes to being both intentional and strategic about leading His children to their destined place.

What exactly is the destined place? According to the dictionary, the word destined means "developing as though according to a plan." Kariger, Brian, Fierro, Daniel. (Dictionary.com, 1995) Interesting enough, we can believe that we are on the road to destiny and be completely off! Here is a throwback for you. How many of you remember MapQuest? MapQuest is a navigation system that is printed from a computer that is used to get the individual using it to their destined place. Personally, I have used it for quite a few road trips when traveling out of town. I can recall on several occasions when using MapQuest that I was more than certain that I was heading in the right direction. Unfortunately for me, I was not always completely on the right path because MapQuest had not detected the roadwork up ahead.

I would get to the place where I was to turn and found myself having to detour based on construction work that was taking place. You could just about imagine that there was a hinge of panic within. Upon approaching the detour sign, I spoke out loud, asking myself, "What should I do?" I was nervous about where I might end up being alone and having several more hours to travel. Unfortunately for me, my cell phone was prior "free" GPS services, so I did not have that service on my phone. I spoke out loud again, saying "Anita, this detour will only take you off your route momentarily and then you'll be back on track sooner than you think!"

Wow! Is that not powerful or what?! Detours only take you off course *momentarily* because it is just a reroute due to an unforeseen situation with the main route. After I spoke those words out loud, I began to calm down. I turned my worship music up a few notches and followed the signs. Following the signs took me in another direction to get me on the right road and that's exactly what God's Positioning System is designed to do. God's way is the only and best way.

> *There is a way which seems right to a man and appears straight before him, but its end is the way of death.*
>
> Proverbs 14:12 (AMP)

We must be willing to obey God's Word because the outcome of our life will only be successful when we do.

I have come face to face with many uncertainties, challenges, and upsets in my life. At one point, I did not think I was emotionally stable enough to make it. I lost heart, my spirit was broken, and I felt like I was forsaken by many, yet I smiled through my personal pain. I still showed up at the building called "church," even though going there did not ease any of the turmoil within. I felt used by some, preyed on by others. I felt that I had been mishandled, not cared for and unattended to. I know that I was left out there in the sea of sharks to do the best I could to not get eaten alive. I could not comprehend much of what was going on apart from the thoughts that God must have been in all of this somehow.

Did I feel Him? Not really. Did I trust Him? Mostly. Was I troubled? Absolutely! Could I find my way to solace again? Yes, and eventually I did. God, in His infinite wisdom, held on to me when I was not holding tightly to Him and navigated my steps, even when I did not know what He was doing.

> *The steps of a [good and righteous] man are directed and established by the Lord; and he delights in his way [and blesses his path].* Psalm 37:23 (AMP)

Interesting enough I felt far from good or righteous. My heart was shattered into pieces, but I masked the brokenness. At times, I felt like God could not possibly love me, but I was a wrong. It was God's love that held me together, gave me strength in my weakest moments, and redirected my path as I knew my heart toward Him was more than others could see. We never land anywhere by accident or coincident. When we are in the Lord and we dedicate our lives to serving and worshiping Him, we will end up where He takes us.

I recall a dream that I had many years ago where I was driving on a mega highway, and I thought I knew the direction I was headed in. Unbeknownst to me, as I was driving, a sign appeared stating, "Go this way." It startled me as I was on my way to take another entrance onto the highway. I followed the sign with great contentment and confidence that the sign would lead me to the place that God had prepared me to be. I awakened from the dream as I was following the sign, and I knew that God was speaking to me. A pure heart cannot be seen by man, but God knows the hearts of those who love Him and will lead and guide them without a doubt.

> *But the Lord said to Samuel, do not look at his appearance or the height of his stature, because I have rejected him. For the Lord sees not as man sees; for man looks at the outward appearance, but the Lord looks at the heart.*
> *1 Samuel 16:7 (AMP)*

I have received many dreams from the Lord since a young age. Most of those dreams I wrote down while many others have been engraved in my spirit and I can recall them just as if I dreamt them yesterday. That dream was my sign to pay attention. God speaks to us in dreams, and in my case, He was letting me know that when I arrived at the fork in the road of life that He would be there to assist me in continuing in the correct direction. God's Positional System works. We will never be steered wrongly. The Bible tells us that the Word of God is as a light that helps us get to where we are going as it relates to our spiritual journey.

> *Your word is a lamp to my feet and a light to my path.*
> *Psalm 119:105 (AMP)*

This scripture lets me know that if I follow the Word and am led by the spirit of God, I cannot lose. It assures me that I will arrive right on time no matter how many delays, detours, or derails come my way; I am going to reach my destined place of promise. You do realize that the children of Israel experienced a forty-year detour and delay. They started out on a journey after which promised to take them to the land promised to them; however, their eleven-day journey to Jericho would take them through the wilderness, wondering around in a circle for four decades. Many of the older generations under the leadership of Moses had died off. Even Moses himself died before he could get to the promised land.

> *Now it happened after the death of Moses the servant of the Lord spoke to Joshua the son of Nun, Moses' my servant (attendant) saying, "Moses My servant is dead; now therefore arise [to take his place], cross over this Jordan, you and all this people into the land which I am giving to them, to the sons of Israel. I have given you every place on which the sole of your foot treads, just as I promised to Moses.* Joshua 1:1-3 (AMP)

This promise from God to the children of Israel and His servants Moses and Joshua was going to happen no matter who was on board. God was being God throughout the entire journey. This means that He heard every complaint, every murmur, knew all doubts and concerns, had foreseen all stumbling blocks and downfalls, knew those who would make and those who would not. My point is that God is with us on our journey, life path, or whatever you deem to call it. If we do not rely on Him, then we are relying on ourselves! We do not order our paths or know the details of our lives and how they will go. We do know as believers that God is our guide. Nothing just happens with God because He is intentional and strategic about His children's lives.

My advice to you, the reader, is to keep your eyes on the Lord. When you fall or lose your way, get up, get back on track, and allow the Lord to redirect and reset you in the spirit of your mind. Never rely on yourself or others to get you to where God has said He is taking you. When God speaks to His children, what happens after that is between them and Him.

I often think about how I thought my life would be. In high school, I was voted the one to be famous. Like many others, I thought that fame was my destiny. I started out singing in third grade, and when my teacher discovered that I could sing, I guess you could say she discovered me. As a result of my singing in the ensemble at my elementary school, I entered talent shows and surprisingly won them. I did not stop there, but I took a shot at pageants and was crowned Miss Talented Teen Cincinnati in 1978 and was first runner up for Miss Talented Teen Ohio my sophomore year of high school. Also in high school, I was given the starring role as Dorothy in *The Wiz*. The show sold out and we had to do an encore performance.

At the age of twenty-two, I did my first studio session, and at twenty-three, Sony records wanted to sign me, but because I had decided that I wanted God more than I wanted a record deal, I forfeited the record deal. I starred in show after show and still did not become famous (at least not in the rich sense). So, what I am saying is that I thought that I was going to be a famous singer/actress living somewhere in another state with a name that would be known across the world. That did not happen!

I will tell you what *did* happen. God, in His infinite wisdom, had a plan for my life. His plan for me included acting, dancing, singing, producing shows, and writing books and literature. God took what He had given me and gave me a choice to use it for His glory. Honestly, I struggled with not taking the path that I desired to take, but the more I have thought about it, I realize that I did not miss anything I thought I desired. I have led thousands of individuals into God's presence all over the country as a worship leader for over thirty years. I have sung background and recorded with several famous individuals. I was blessed to be in a scene of *Alex Cross* starring Tyler Perry and the list goes on. All I am trying to convey is that God knows the road we are to take, and many times, we veer off, taking another path that seems right.

Many plans are in a man's mind, but it is the Lord's purpose for him that will stand (be carried out).
                                                    Proverbs 19:21 (AMP)

God's Positioning System (GPS)

God's plan for my life so far has been carried out, with a few detours along the way. I honestly thought that I had missed God on a few occasions, but be it as it may, I did not miss Him because He knew what was ahead of me before I even arrived to it.

I recall the year one of my favorite cousins died suddenly. I was on my way to Florida when I received the news. Upon receiving this devastating news, I was trying to figure out how I could leave Florida and go to Atlanta the day of the funeral then return to Florida. My family and I put our heads together and purchased a ticket for me to attend my cousin's funeral. The morning of the funeral, I was a mess. I was dropped off at the airport for check-in and anxiously awaited my flight. This was a hard one, considering that my only brother was murdered a few years prior to my cousin's untimely death. The time came for me to board my flight and a message was sent over the intercom that the flight was delayed for forty-five minutes to an hour due to mechanical issues.

This put me in a tizzy, so to speak. I was already a mess and just wanted this part to be over with. I informed my ride that I was still at the airport due to a delay of the flight. The time finally was close for me to board and strangely enough, there was a second announcement stating that my flight would still be delayed due to there still being mechanical issues. At this point, I was not going to make it to the funeral to say my good-byes. I was not good at all. I cried and cried. I was sad and disappointed that I could not get to Atlanta, and then it hit me like a brick that God was sparing my life! Had the mechanics not sighted the mechanical errors, I would have undoubtably been on that plane and could have possibly been buried right after my cousin.

God never fails when it comes to directing life's traffic. He alone is the best Traffic Controller! He directs on purpose and with purpose. He tells us which way to go and how to get there, and I am so very thankful that God is continuing the work that He began in me many years ago, just like He is completing the work in each of you! Follow the path that God has carved out for you and trust Him to get you there.

> *Trust in the Lord with all thine heart; lean not unto thine all understanding. In all thy ways acknowledge him, and he shall direct thy paths.* Proverbs 3:5-6 (KJV)

Chapter 5

God's Plan

Perhaps you can relate to having had pain—be it physical or emotional—that seemingly would not leave no matter what you did or what somebody said to you. Personally, I can attest to having this unbelievable kind of pain. I had it and did not know what to do with it. My heart had been trampled upon and my spirit had been broken. My breathing was labored, and, at times, living was a chore, yet I would always find a way to see God in it all. Did you know that God is in the details? Yes, He is! The details of our lives matter to God. God is always concerned

I found myself hanging on by the knot that I had tied at the end of my rope. I tied it big enough because I desired with what little strength, I had to hang on to my life no matter how much pain I was in, which was a lot. You see, "divorce" happens over time, but it manifests itself throughout the years. Divorce does not happen overnight, is what I am saying.

By the time we arrived at the date on the divorce decree, so much damage had already been done. I was weary with the details of what had started wrong. In my case, it started wrong, and I had lived with how wrong things were for many years just to end up divorced, vulnerable, afraid, and feeling very alone. I want to be clear that I place no blame on anyone but the Enemy. It was the Enemy (Satan) who was given room to slide in, working the sidelines doing what he does best, dividing and conquering.

My plan was to leave the state where I grew up and relocate to Tennessee. I did not make it there because I found myself in a situation that crushed my spirit even more. I was so low on myself that I accepted any kind of treatment, which resulted in me getting involved with someone too soon after my divorce. I was nowhere close to being ready to be in a relationship, but be it as it may, I tricked myself into believing that it was safe. Afterall, he was someone I had known to be a decent person. Well, let me just say that my life was flipped upside down for over a year. I was still healing from the divorce when along came another major crash! The lies, deceit, words spoken to me and about me to others as well as the horrible games played almost caused me to die a slow death spiritually. I was on a downward spiral, and I fought to survive the best way I knew how.

There were many unexpected things that took place in my life during the first few years after being on my own. I met new people and God revamped my entire life! What I am saying is that He changed things within based on the challenges that I had faced. A revamp is to give new and improved form, structure, or appearance to. Murray, James, Sir (The Oxford English Dictionary, 1879) In other words, He renovated me. I was under construction. I felt things being shaved off. I could tell that God was turning things around. I knew that when my friend circle shifted, things were really shifting.

I struggled with accepting my new life. I didn't know how to move away from the pain of rejection. We all know that rejection is no joke; after all, many of us grow up experiencing some forms of rejection. I was no different. I was in lots of pain, crushed beyond repair. I had always had a prayer life, but I found prayer difficult to do, until by divine order I was asked out by a friend to go to the movies. I really did not want to go because I was recovering from foot surgery, which was a difficult surgery to go through. I was on crutches and in a boot that had an apparatus that stuck out of the top of my foot, which caused me so much pain. I equated the pain in my foot to the pain in my heart because they were equal in how they made me feel.

Regardless, I decided to go with my friend to see the movie *War Room*, a 2015 movie about a couple, who were believers, who were experiencing difficult times in their marriage. Interesting enough, they managed to somehow find themselves at the crossroad with their marital relationship, as many married couples do (I knew that place oh so well). I had gone through a divorce, just to be hurt all over again nine months later. I really did not understand what was going on, but I knew that something had to change: me! And little did I know after seeing that movie that my prayer life was going to be revived as well as taken to an entirely new level, and that I would see forgiveness, God's love, grace, and mercy from an entirely new perspective. I had no choice, but to shift in my spirit because I was stuck!

We arrived at the theater where the movie was showing, and I sat comfortably in my seat, anticipating what was to come. The movie started and I was instantly drawn in by the story line because I had been there. I watched the movie with such intensity, expecting that I would take something away from it. Undoubtably, saying that I took something away from it is an understatement because the movie saved me. It caused me to push through until the heaviness broke off of me. I was given no choice but to rise from where I had found myself, because at that time ,life was hard on me and all I wanted to do was stop the pain.I know you know what I am talking about, so you know I had no choice but to go to the movies as God used my friend to get me there.

The movie arrived at the point where the wife was so frustrated with how things were going, and she did more emotionalizing the situation than anything else. Isn't that the case with many of us? We try to fight these spiritual battles with carnal weaponry. That will not work! She found out quickly that the flesh could not handle the things of the spirit and that she had to do some things differently if she wanted different results. As the movie proceeded with the frustrated wife, who happened to be a realtor, meeting a potential seller, this meeting was no accident. God already knew that the frustrated wife needed the likings of the prayer warrior who was selling her home; after all, the seller was no stranger to God, His Word, or prayer. She walked in the spirit and in God's authority. I can only imagine that this seasoned woman had encountered many battles and celebrated many victories won at the hands of her Father God! God deliberately causes us to triumph by seeing that we get to the other side of the storm. He was deliberate about my healing, my restoration, and my success in Him!

The movie was getting heavy. The realtor met a woman who knew who she was in God. She did not play with the things of God and her boldness in the Lord was an obvious trait. When the two meet each other, things begin to happen. Both of their lives are changed for the better and neither of them would ever be the same.

The premise of the movie is that prayer works. After the realtor, who was introduced to prayer by the woman who was selling her home, she witnessed how the power of prayer changed her and would ultimately change her marriage for the better.

I knew, without a doubt, that God purposed for me to see this movie. I was ready for the change to take place in me. I did not want to hurt anymore, cry anymore, feel ashamed anymore, be taunted anymore, feel rejected or dejected anymore, and I most certainly did not want to carry the pain of my past anymore. I had had enough!

After the movie was over, I remained silent. The ride home was quiet. I did express my gratitude to my friend for inviting me to go see the movie as well as for picking me up; after all, I was on crutches due to having surgery on my foot and was feeling a bit down. I had so many thoughts going through my head, I must admit, but the main thought taking up space in my brain was, "I must get there. I must get this heaviness off of me," and it would only happen through the power of prayer. Essentially, I was no stranger to prayer. I had a prayer life. I was just too emotionally scarred to sincerely pray and let it go. When I did pray, I held on to it until I was reminded of how effective the power of prayer is when it's left in the hands of Jesus.

We are told in the Word of God to pray and not faint. This scripture is found in Luke 1:18 when Jesus is speaking to His disciples in the form of a parable. Story or fable, He warns them that the world is going to get worse and that the only way to not experience spiritual unconsciousness is to *pray*! I was just on the brink of fainting because of my scuffle with prayer when God spoke to my brokenness through the movie, and I was able to break through from where I had been for too long. My life changed immediately, and I was ready for things to be different!

As time passed, I felt better, but I still needed something more to happen, and one day, it did. I was walking through my apartment while cleaning. There was not a lot on my mind except for getting to finish my chores. I had just about completed everything when out of nowhere, I fell to my knees. I mean, I fell hard and the items in my hand hit the floor while I buckled over, grasping my core as I wailed out! I wept for close to an hour, praying for relief from the heaviness I carried. I had carried it for quite some time and it was more than I could bear. That was the moment I released everything. I could not get up off of the floor until I let go, forgave, and allowed God to fill my heart and that apartment with His multiplied grace and peace (2 Peter 1:2). I felt lighter, better, and I knew that my healing was in progress.

I found myself desiring to pray as I once did, so I scheduled my prayer time. Yes, you heard me right, I wrote in my planner a scheduled appointment time with God just like I used to do; after all, my thinking was that we schedule appointments for everything else. We schedule doctors' appointments, workout classes, shopping sprees, hair and nail appointments, vacation schedules; we pretty much schedule everything of importance, but not many people think about scheduling time with God. It works for me! Spending time in prayer, worship, and God's Word is not a part of my life, but it is my life!

After that day of renewal, I have not looked back. I am so thankful that God had me on His mind enough to use a movie to realign me and remind me that He has a plan for my life. There are so many ways God will use when it comes to delivering His children. I remember hearing older people say, "There is more than one way to skin a cat." My take from that is that there is no one absolute way to make things happen. And so it is with God's plans for us. He will do whatever He needs to do to keep us on track that we may fulfill destiny.

I will be forever grateful for the events that God, in His infinite wisdom and strength, snatched before my train jumped the track and put be back on the road that led to peace, joy, success, victory, deliverance, and hope. Yes, you may be exactly where I was all those years ago, but I promise you if you are willing to yield to God's plans for you, it will absolutely come to pass. I want to remind you that your course in life is not finished until you complete it. When God allows you and I another day of life, you can trust that His plan for us is still in motion. There is a song that I love so very much called "He's Able" by Deitrick Haddon & Voices of Unity. The lyrics provide such powerful words, and what a promise to know that God wants to fulfill the plan that He has for our lives and that all we humans must do is yield!

Honestly, it can be challenging to yield to God when you can't comprehend what it is that He is doing. I am a planner by nature. I prefer that everything about my life be organized because I function better. For as long as I can remember, I have kept planners, calendars, and have used a multiplicity of gadgets to help keep me organized. When I was in college, I kept several planners. When I became a mother to two young daughters, I kept everything written on a calendar and my planner concerning their upcoming appointments and other important dates. When I started teaching, I wrote out and kept daily to-do lists that served the purpose of knowing what my day would entail. I also had a physical calendar on my desk that helped me with reminders of important dates and deadlines that must be met. As a worship leader, I plan when I will send out songs, how long we will work on them, and the Sunday when we will present the songs to the congregation.

I think you get my drift, but no matter how much I was able to plan for the things I did daily, I could have never planned my future according to what God already had in mind for me. God's plan for my life is inclusive of my experiencing some highs and lows, some tears and laughter, some ups and downs, and some victories and defeats! And I am here to speak about it and to help someone who may be in the eye of their storm and feeling like they are being tossed around like debris.

If, in fact, that's you, I want to remind you that storms eventually pass. Yours is about to be over with soon. It may not feel like it, but your trouble will soon be over. God's plan is to develop us, and it is during the toughest times of our lives that development begins. Trouble will either push us closer to God or push us away from Him. We will either learn to pray or we will become prayerless. We will either trust God or we will trust our own instincts. Storms typically bring destruction and have the propensity to tear up and tear down whatever is there when it lands. In fact, storms often destroy to the point of having to rebuild and reestablish, which can be a horrific process, but when it's all over and all things are made new, there is no sign that a storm ravaged a place. Do you recall some of the natural disasters that have wreaked havoc turning cities, states, and even some countries upside down? Is this not what is happening in our lives as believers? When life happens because God permits it to, if we allow God to fix us up after the storm, there is no evidence of a storm.

And after you have suffered a little while, the God of all grace, who has called you to his eternal Glory in Christ, will himself restore, confirm, strengthen and establish you. 1 Peter 5:10 (ESV)

I love the Word of God! There is an answer for every question and a solution to every problem. It is God who permits the storm to come, but then that same God who did not allow us to perish in the storm puts us back together and, as a result, we are better than ever. It is about God's plan!

Chapter 6

Healing Comes from the Lord

I feel it necessary and am much led to speak to those of you who are experiencing life right now. No, I am not referring to the grander parts of life, I am speaking about the parts of life that caused you to crash because it happened so suddenly. As difficult as it may be for you now, you are going to rise from your current situation. Do you know that all of the promises in God are "Yes" and "Amen"? Of course, that is not easy to remember when you believe you will not make it, cannot stop crying, and cannot stop hurting. I was there; therefore, I need to encourage your soul right at this very moment as those individuals God has used during my Lo-debar moments encouraged me!

My healing was starting to take place. It was not easy, but I needed all of my open wounds to be closed. Jesus had His work cut out for Him when it came to helping me let go of the things that I believed were impossible to let go of, but I eventually did. I will not tell you that things got easier immediately because they did not. In the beginning of my healing, I struggled to remember all of the good and how to forget all of the bad! That's a no brainer. That's how we humans are wired. In most instances, we are quick to recall and hold on to the things that caused us the most misery rather than focusing on the things that made us feel happy, loved, wanted, appreciated, and special!

I had to be intentional about the time that I spent in the Word of God, in prayer, and attending worship gatherings. I had good days and I had bad days. I had some very dark days and I had many bright day that felt hopeful. What was most important for me was to stop looking back and to remember that God is the Mender of broken hearts.

I recall on one of my dark days that I was driving home, feeling so heavy. I wanted to cry and scream all at the same time. It was a very low place. While driving, I was listening to my favorite radio station WAKW 93.3 when a song that I had not heard before began to play. I recall the first few lines of the first stanza causing me to burst into tears. The name of the song was "Tell Your Heart to Beat Again" by Danny Gokey. I remember thinking to myself as the song was filling the entire space of my little car as well as my entire body, "This song is speaking life to me."

With tears flooding my eyes and running down my neck and onto the front of my jacket, I pulled into the driveway, parked my car, and broke. I broke in ways I had not before after hearing this song. You see, spiritually, my heart had become faint and needed to be revived, resuscitated, and be given spiritual CPR. I needed my spiritual heart to connect to my natural heart so that I would remain alive. I wanted to live and not die. I needed to speak to my wounded and broken spirit and to demand my heart, by faith, to beat again! And I did just that. I managed to get out of my car and into my apartment where I dropped to my knees and, with everything in me, told my heart to beat again! I spoke to my inner man and told it to live and breathe again. Finally, I spoke to God and asked Him to revive me and to make me whole. And He did just that.

God had spoken to me through the words of that powerful song. That was it! That was what I had been waiting for. The song did not just enter my ears, but it went down into the basement of my soul and connected with my spirit, instructing me to live! Those life-changing lyrics in conjunction with the Holy Spirit shifted my entire being. After I got up from the floor, I searched for the song, found it, and listened to it repeatedly. I kept saying out loud, "This song was written just for me." Yes, Danny Gokey may have written it from a place where he had once been, but this song was for Anita!

At that very moment, I was resuscitated! My spiritual heart began to beat again. The strength of God could be felt. I could feel my spirit being lifted. God lifted me out of that place that was so dark and set me back on a steady path, just like He did with King David in Psalm 40.

> *I waited patiently and expectantly for the Lord; and He inclined to me and heard my cry. He brought me up out of a horrible pit [of tumult and destruction], out of the miry clay, and He set my feet upon a rock, steadying my footsteps and establishing my path. He put a new song in my mouth, a song of praise to our God; Many will see and fear [with great reverence] and will trust confidently in the Lord.* Psalm 40:1-3 (AMP)

I can now say, without a doubt, that it was in God's plan that I heard that song on that day at the time. It was just another added piece to propelling my healing in progress.

I want to remind you that nothing happens by chance or happenstance in God. As believers, if we trust God for and with our lives, we will always be able to testify to the fact that God always carries us through our difficult circumstances and brings us out to a victorious place. I had to trust God in that broken and crushed place just like you must do. Healing comes when we realize that we need it. I had to acknowledge out of my own mouth that I needed God and that if He did not heal me, I could not be healed. It is for that reason alone that I am walking in total healing today.

Then the word of the Lord came to Jeremiah the second time, while he was still confined in the court of the guard, saying, "Thus says the Lord who made the earth, the Lord who formed it to establish it-the Lord is His name. 'Call to Me and I will answer you and tell you [and even show you] great and mighty things, [things which have been confined and hidden], which you do not know and understand and cannot distinguish... Behold, [in the restored Jerusalem] I will bring health and healing, and I will heal them; and I will reveal to them an abundance of peace (prosperity, security, stability) and truth.

Jeremiah 33:1-3, 6 (AMP)

Wow! That's our God! And that's not only who He is, but also what He does! He hears our cries of desperation and inclines His ear to us when we call Him in truth! Prayer truth is the best truth. When we call out to God (as I did while I was in a destitute place asking for help), He hears us, brings us out, dusts us off, cleans us up, wipes away our tears, fortifies our spirit, gives us an oil and lube change, realigns us, gets the kinks out, wipes our slate clean, and heals our souls. Yes! Healing is for you and me! We do not have to stay in Lo-debar; we can come out healed and walk in an abundance of peace, prosperity, security, and stability!

When I think about what it means to be healed, I immediately think of forgiveness. That may sound a little strange however, when we are seeking complete healing of the spirit, soul and body forgiveness must be sought after. Afterall when Jesus healed the sick, in most cases he forgave them of their sins.

One day Jesus was teaching, and Pharisees and teachers of the Law were sitting there. They had come from every village of Galilee and from Judea and Jerusalem. And the power of the Lord was with Jesus to heal the sick. Some men came carrying a paralyzed man on a mat and tried to take him into the house to lay him before Jesus. When they could not find a way to do this because of the crowd, they went up on the roof and lowered him on his mat through the tiles into the middle of the crowd, right in front of Jesus. When Jesus saw their faith, he said, "Friend, your sins are forgiven." Luke 5:17 -20 (NIV)

You may ask why Jesus forgave the man of his sins in order that he be healed. Based on what I have studied, there could possibly be a two-fold reason as to why Jesus did not just heal them and leave it at that. First, some Bible scholars believe that Jesus chose to forgive people's sins when performing miracles because He wanted them to see that not even their sins would stop Him from healing them. Second, at that time, many people who were afflicted with disease thought that sin was the cause of disease, and when Jesus let them know that He'd forgiven them and healed them, it was miraculous and evidence to the religious leaders that He really was the Son of God and that He had authority to heal.

Let's fast forward to 2021. I have had to forgive much! I have had to forgive even when the ones who hurt me did not ask for forgiveness or admit to their wrongdoing. Why did I forgive? Because I have been forgiven of much! My life has not been perfect, and I have not done all things right, so I've needed forgiveness a multiplicity of times. The word forgiveness in Greek is *Metonia*, which means "repentance, change intentions, change of heart and mind." Please understand that forgiveness and repentance go hand in hand. Strongs Greek and Hebrew Online Lexicon. (EliYah Ministries, 1995)

Who is a God like you, who pardons sins and forgives the transgressions of the remnant of his inheritance?
                                        Micah 7:18 (NIV)

This is what the Sovereign Lord, the Holy Ones of Israel says: In repentance and rest is salvation, in quietness and trust your strength, but you would have none of it. Isaiah 30:15 (NIV)

Peter said to them, "Each one of you must turn away from your and be baptized in the name of the Lord Jesus Christ, so that your sins will be forgive; and you shall receive God's gift of the Holy Spirit. Acts 2:38 (NLT)

Whether is it easier to say to the sick of palsy, Thy sins be forgiven thee, or to say Arise and take up thy bed, and walk? Mark 2:9 (KJV)

I think you get it. Forgiveness and repentance are directly connected; you can't have one without the other.

I have learned on this journey of life that being hurt and disappointed by others will happen and can sometimes result in one having deep wounds as well as finding it difficult to forgive those who caused the pain. But forgiveness can and will take place and can only be obtained from a genuine desire to be forgiven. Then comes forgiveness and a life lived of freedom from holding others hostage to move forward in healing. Healing is necessary! When one is healed, they see, hear, and do things differently. Healed people help heal while hurting people tend to hurt. James 5:16 speaks of confessing our sins one to another that we may be healed and restored. The Greek word for healed in this text is *Eeahomahee*, which means "heal, or make whole." In that same verse, we are encouraged to openly confess our faults to one another. The word faults in the Greek is *Paraptoma*, which means "a side slip, lapse or deviation, error, transgression, fall, fault, offence, sin or trespass." The Greek ad Hebrew Online Lexicon. (EliYah Ministries, 1995)

The ability to confess faults, errors, and slip ups ultimately helps heal us. As we heal, we forgive and let go! I am in no way saying that we forget; it is virtually impossible to forget unless our brains sustain injury or disease. The brain stores and files material just like a computer. The hard drive of a computer stores all of the data from files to software and this, too, is how our brain functions. It stores and files memories from childhood on into adulthood, so when we need those files, they are available for usage. My point is that we may not ever forget the hurt and pain inflicted upon us by others, but the pain will become less to the point of being obsolete as we walk in our restored place of healing and wholeness!

Allow God's healing virtue to flow to you. Do not let another year, month, week, day, hour, minute or second go by where you do not receive your healing. Healing is yours and mines. I found 102 scriptures of healing in the Bible. Some refer to spiritual healing. Some are for physical healings. Then there are the scriptures that speak to our emotional healing. Why? Because we are tri-part beings and God is concerned about our entire being, not just our souls.

God forgives, God heals, God restores! Be healed and stay healed!

CHAPTER 7

Renewed Strength

It's interesting that as I look back and reflect on some of the most difficult parts of my journey, I know that God was always with me. In those moments of weakness when I did not think I would ever smile or laugh again, let alone want to, I know, without a doubt, that it is God who brought me to this very pivotal place that I am at as well as given me renewed strength and a different outlook on life. My vision was blurred during those times and could not see clearly.

You know that if something must be renewed, it means that it needs to be extended or done over. The word renew means to resume after an interruption. Murray, William, Sir. (Oxford Online Dictionary, 1839). I like that definition because it speaks for itself. There had been interruptions that took away what I term to be strength. I was depleted of energy, life, hope and I had no vigor. I was so weak and only wanted to feel like myself again. God did it! What did He do? I am so glad you asked. He renewed my strength and brought total and complete restoration to my weary soul!

What does it mean to be weary? It means you are tired. Weary, when used as an adjective, means feeling or showing tiredness, especially because of excessive exertion or lack of sleep. Murray, William, Sir. (Oxford Online Dictionary, 1839). It also means fatigued, taxed, or drained. After being in that place of exhaustion, I know that God was able to bring me to a better place than what I had previously been in. Finally, I was beginning to feel better about myself and about life in general. I was having more up days than down. I felt the pep return to my step and life was getting better.

Was everything all good with me? No. Was there still residue from the things I had gone through? Yes. Did I desire to continue pushing through and trusting that God was going to fix me completely up and restore me? Yes and yes! Problems, pain, struggle, faults, failures, disappointments, or fatigue did not consume me, and I am so grateful to God that it didn't.

> *It is of the Lord's mercies that we are not consumed, because his compassions fail not. They are new every morning: great is thy faithfulness.*
> *Lamentations 3:22-23 (KJV)*

God is faithful when nothing or no one else is. I should have been consumed! I could have perished amid all that was happening, but the Lord Jehovah-Nissi protected me just like He did on many accounts with the children of Israel! It is in the Book of Exodus where we get to be an eyewitness of God's mercy, protection, and restoration with Moses and the children of Israel:

> *And the Lord said unto Moses, write this for a memorial in a book, and rehearse it in the ears of Joshua: for I will utterly put out the remembrance of Amalek from under heaven. And Moses built an altar and called the name of it Jehovahnissi: For he said, Because the Lord hath sworn that the Lord will have war with Amalek from generation to generation. Exodus 17:14-16 (KJV)*

Printed in Great Britain
by Amazon